Library of Congress Cataloging-in-Publication Data

Schuster, Fred E.
　　Employee-centered management : a strategy for high commitment and
involvement / Frederick E. Schuster.
　　　　p.　cm.
　　Includes bibliographical references and index.
　　ISBN 1-56720-187-3 (alk. paper)
　　1. Industrial managment.　I. Title.
　　HD31.S341563　　1998
　　658.3—dc21　　　　97-41003

British Library Cataloguing in Publication Data is available.

Library of Congress Catalog Card Number: 97-41003
ISBN: 1-56720-187-3

First published in 1998

Quorum Books, 88 Post Road West, Westport, CT 06881
An imprint of Greenwood Publishing Group, Inc.

Printed in the United States of America

The paper used in this book complies with the
Permanent Paper Standard issued by the National
Information Standards Organization (Z39.48-1984).

10　9　8　7　6　5　4　3　2　1